Golden Screens 2025

*Inside the Year's Biggest Emmy
Nominations and TV Triumphs*

Jackson E. Carter

Follow for more reviews, book updates, and behind-the-scenes content:
Instagram: @globalwriterbooks
TikTok: @globalwriterbooks

Table of contents

Introduction

A Golden Year of Television Excellence

Television in 2025 is more than entertainment—it's a cultural force, a mirror of society, and a driver of conversation around the world. As audiences continue to evolve alongside technology, the small screen has expanded its reach and deepened its impact, creating space for stories that are more diverse, daring, and dynamic than ever before. In this dazzling ecosystem of streaming giants, cable cornerstones, and network stalwarts, the Primetime Emmy® Awards remain the industry's most coveted honor, spotlighting excellence across drama, comedy, limited series, reality TV, and beyond.

Golden Screens 2025 is a deep dive into this year's Emmy nominations—an essential companion for fans, critics, and curious minds alike. This book unpacks the standout shows, game-changing performances, behind-the-scenes breakthroughs, and unforgettable moments that led to this season's most celebrated nominations. From record-breaking new contenders to emotional returns from fan favorites, the 77th Emmy Awards reflect a fascinating snapshot of where television stands today—and where it may be headed next.

This year's nominations speak volumes about the evolving landscape of television. Traditional boundaries between genres are blurring. Hybrid shows—like The Bear, which masterfully blends dark comedy with heartfelt drama—are not just being accepted, they're dominating. Meanwhile, streaming services continue to flex their muscles, offering high-concept, big-budget productions that rival cinema. Severance, for instance, with its cerebral plot and artistic vision, led the field with an astounding 27 nominations. It proved that audiences are eager to be challenged and that narrative complexity can thrive in a binge-worthy format.

Newcomers also made a dramatic entrance. The Studio, a satire about the inner workings of a Hollywood production company, tied a record for a freshman comedy series by landing 23 nominations. It's a bold reminder that fresh voices and original premises still have a place in a crowded market. Similarly, The Penguin showcased a striking transformation of the superhero genre, turning a familiar comic book character into a gritty antihero in a limited series format that racked up 24 nominations.

While streaming continues to dominate the awards conversation, network television hasn't disappeared from the narrative. Shows like Abbott Elementary and The Daily Show represent the enduring power of broadcast to connect, educate, and amuse. In the reality and variety space, series like RuPaul's Drag Race, The Traitors, and Top Chef continue to redefine what excellence looks like in unscripted television.

This year's Emmy contenders aren't just creatively impressive—they're socially significant. More than ever, representation matters. Nominees include a broader range of voices across race, gender identity, sexuality, and cultural background. Performers like Bella Ramsey (The Last of Us), Bowen Yang (Saturday Night Live), and Colman Domingo (Rustin, Euphoria) reflect an industry slowly but surely embracing the full spectrum of human experience. These nods aren't simply token inclusions; they're recognition of undeniable talent and the richness that diverse storytelling brings to the screen.

Another striking trend of 2025 is the celebration of complexity in characters and themes. Audiences and critics alike are rewarding shows that resist easy answers. Slow Horses dives into the moral ambiguity of intelligence work; The Diplomat explores the cost of public service through a feminist lens; and Paradise presents a gripping, near-future political thriller that hits startlingly close to home. These nominations tell us that prestige TV is no longer content with just compelling characters—it now seeks to provoke thought, ignite dialogue, and challenge convention.

Beyond the nominated shows themselves, this Emmy season is also shaped by the industry's broader context. The aftermath of the 2023–2024 Hollywood strikes, shifts in streaming business models, and ongoing debates about AI's role in content creation have all impacted the production and distribution of television. Despite these challenges, 2025's nominees reflect a resilient industry finding new ways to innovate. Creators are responding to uncertainty not with hesitation but with courage, pushing creative boundaries and experimenting with form, tone, and platform.

Golden Screens 2025 doesn't just list the nominations—it unpacks them. Throughout this book, we'll explore why certain performances resonated, how production teams elevated their craft, and what makes specific episodes worthy of Emmy gold. Each chapter focuses on a major category or trend, from lead acting races to the best in limited series and comedy. We'll spotlight breakout stars, dissect award-season strategies, and even look at surprising snubs and omissions that sparked conversation and controversy.

This book is also a celebration. It honors the labor of countless writers, directors, editors, performers, and crew members who poured passion into their work. The Emmy nominations serve as a validation of that effort, even when they stir debate or disappointment. They remind us that television is a collective art form, one shaped by collaboration as much as by vision.

Whether you're a casual viewer curious about what's worth watching or a diehard awards-season follower, this guide will help you appreciate the craft behind the content. It's an invitation to look beyond the glamour of the red carpet and into the storytelling, risk-taking, and relentless work that make Emmy recognition meaningful.

So grab your remote—or more likely, your streaming queue—and prepare to revisit the shows that shaped 2025's television landscape. From laugh-out-loud comedies to gut-wrenching dramas and genre-defying hybrids, Golden Screens 2025 is your backstage pass to the best of television's brightest night.

Chapter 1

The Rise of Prestige Streaming

The 2025 Emmy nominations have underscored one undeniable truth: streaming has become not just a dominant platform for television consumption, but the breeding ground for prestige content that redefines the medium itself. This year's awards season has been shaped by a new class of streaming titans whose work challenges traditional structures, invites intellectual curiosity, and captivates global audiences. With shows like Severance, The Penguin, The Studio, and Paradise leading the pack, it's clear that the streaming revolution has matured into something far more refined—an engine for award-winning artistry and storytelling excellence.

The defining case of streaming dominance is Severance, which returned with its much-anticipated second season and led all nominations with a staggering 27 nods. Produced by Apple TV+, the show exemplifies what modern prestige television can achieve when platform freedom meets visionary creativity. Directed by Ben Stiller and created by Dan Erickson, Severance is set in a sterile, dystopian workplace where employees undergo a surgical procedure to separate their work and personal memories. This high-concept premise is executed with profound emotional weight and social commentary, touching on corporate dehumanization, personal identity, and the very nature of consciousness. The show's visual precision, eerie world-building, and haunting performances—particularly from Adam Scott and Britt Lower—have cemented it as one of the era's most intellectually ambitious dramas.

What sets Severance apart is how it embodies the best of what streaming allows: risky storytelling that isn't rushed by ratings, serialized complexity that unfolds gradually, and high production value that doesn't compromise thematic depth. Apple TV+ has positioned itself as a serious contender in the streaming landscape, and Severance proves that investment in quality over quantity can pay off in both critical acclaim and audience loyalty.

Meanwhile, HBO Max (soon to be simply "Max") offered its own contender for Emmy glory with The Penguin, a limited series spun off from Matt

Reeves' 2022 film The Batman. Starring Colin Farrell in a transformative, prosthetics-heavy role, The Penguin dives into the grimy criminal underworld of Gotham with surprising narrative sophistication. Gone are the days when comic book adaptations were relegated to pop spectacle—The Penguin is steeped in character-driven drama, exploring themes of power, identity, and the trauma of legacy. It is noir television with Shakespearean ambition, shot with cinematic grit and elevated by top-tier direction, costume design, and a standout score.

What's particularly remarkable about The Penguin is how it takes genre storytelling and pushes it into Emmy territory. Much like Watchmen did in 2019 or The Mandalorian more recently, this series proves that superhero-adjacent content can evolve into something prestigious when it's approached with literary ambition and artistic discipline. HBO Max has long maintained a reputation for quality through its original programming, but with The Penguin, it has extended its reach into the realm of franchise storytelling with prestige credibility.

Another show turning heads is The Studio, a freshman comedy from Netflix that tied a record for most nominations by a new series—23 in total. A behind-the-scenes satire of Hollywood's creative chaos, The Studio blends sharp wit with biting commentary about the entertainment industry. It's a show that feels tailor-made for awards season: layered, funny, self-aware, and anchored by brilliant performances from Seth Rogen, Maya Rudolph, and a surprising dramatic turn from Kristen Wiig.

Streaming's success at the Emmys is not just about individual shows—it's about the infrastructure behind them. These platforms have reshaped how television is developed, greenlit, and consumed. Creators now have the freedom to build complex universes without the pressure of immediate ratings or advertiser appeasement. The serialized nature of streaming allows for slow-burn storytelling that respects the viewer's intelligence. And the global reach of these platforms means that buzz can grow organically across markets, turning niche series into international sensations seemingly overnight.

Beyond Apple TV+ and HBO Max, services like Hulu, Amazon Prime Video, and Netflix continue to exert massive influence. The Bear (Hulu) and Shrinking (Apple TV+) have shown that even in the crowded comedy space, streaming series can balance levity with emotional gravity. Amazon's The

Diplomat has attracted praise for its geopolitical tension and layered female protagonist, while Netflix's anthology Black Mirror returned with episodes that stunned and unsettled in equal measure. Each of these shows contributes to a larger narrative: that the best storytelling is now more likely to emerge from a streamer than a traditional network.

Of course, this shift hasn't come without consequences. As streaming platforms chase prestige, they've also created intense competition for viewer attention. With dozens of new series debuting every month, even critically acclaimed shows can get buried without the right promotion or platform visibility. Additionally, the ever-changing economics of streaming have raised concerns about sustainability, especially as platforms consolidate, cut budgets, or cancel beloved shows after a single season.

Still, from a creative standpoint, the results are undeniable. Streaming has elevated television from a medium once dominated by episodic procedural formulas into a space where experimentation thrives. Shows like Severance and The Penguin would have struggled to find footing in the cable model of the early 2000s. Now, they are at the forefront of what audiences expect from award-worthy TV—smart, stylish, and subversive.

This year's Emmys have also proven that streaming success isn't just about spectacle. Shows like Paradise, a political thriller set in a fictional African republic, and Slow Horses, a British spy series from Apple TV+, demonstrate that performance, writing, and pacing matter just as much as production value. Streaming has given international stories a platform and elevated niche genres to global relevance. This democratization of content has leveled the playing field and broadened the scope of what constitutes "prestige" TV.

In many ways, the streaming era has brought television closer to cinema than ever before. Limited series like The Penguin feel like multi-part films, complete with Oscar-level performances and production. Directors like Cary Joji Fukunaga, Barry Jenkins, and Reed Morano have all crossed from film into TV, blurring the lines between the mediums. In 2025, the Emmy nomination list reads like a prestigious film festival program—testament to how far television has come and how essential streaming has become to its growth.

Looking ahead, the rise of prestige streaming raises key questions: Will the Emmy Awards continue to favor platforms with the deepest pockets? Can smaller or independent creators break through? How will industry strikes, cost-cutting measures, and AI-driven disruptions affect the future of prestige TV? These questions linger, but one thing is clear: streaming is not just a platform—it is the new foundation of elite television.

The 2025 Emmy season has etched this reality into stone. With shows like Severance, The Penguin, The Studio, and Paradise leading the way, the era of prestige streaming is not only here—it's thriving, evolving, and rewriting what it means to be award-worthy. For audiences and creators alike, that means more daring stories, more ambitious formats, and more reasons to fall in love with television all over again.

Chapter 2

The Battle for Best Drama Series

Each Emmy season brings its own wave of competitive energy, but few categories ignite anticipation like Outstanding Drama Series. In 2025, this coveted field is a testament to the creative depth, cultural relevance, and cinematic ambition of modern television. With nominees like Severance, The White Lotus, The Last of Us, The Diplomat, Slow Horses, Andor, Paradise, and The Pitt, the drama category reflects a thrilling range of themes—from post-apocalyptic survival to political espionage to surreal workplace horror. These shows are not just contenders; they are landmarks in storytelling, each pushing the boundaries of what the small screen can achieve.

Leading the charge is Severance (Apple TV+), which returns to the category as a frontrunner with its mind-bending concept and haunting execution. Its blend of psychological horror and dystopian satire has not only captivated audiences but also gained critical acclaim for its layered narrative and visual storytelling. Adam Scott's portrayal of Mark Scout—a man navigating life with a surgically divided consciousness—has earned him a Lead Actor nomination, while the show's eerie production design and meticulous editing secured technical nods. What makes Severance a standout is its ability to feel both timely and timeless. It taps into the alienation of corporate culture while presenting a mystery that deepens with every scene. It's not just about solving a puzzle—it's about confronting what makes us human.

Joining Severance is The White Lotus (Max), the anthology series created by Mike White that continues to evolve with each season. The latest installment shifts its focus to Southeast Asia, weaving tales of wealth, desire, and cultural tension among an elite group of vacationers. The show's signature blend of dark humor and existential dread is on full display, with lush visuals and a creeping sense of doom that builds to a powerful conclusion. The White Lotus doesn't just entertain—it provokes. It invites viewers to consider privilege, power dynamics, and the fragile façade of affluence. Its third Emmy run proves that White's creation is not a one-time wonder, but a series capable of sustained brilliance.

Another strong contender is The Last of Us (HBO), the video game adaptation that has shattered expectations. What could have been another post-apocalyptic story instead became an emotional epic, with Pedro Pascal and Bella Ramsey delivering performances that elevate the genre. Set in a world ravaged by fungal infection and societal collapse, The Last of Us explores the enduring bonds of love, loyalty, and survival. It's violent and tender, expansive and intimate. The series stands out not only for its faithful yet inventive adaptation, but also for the sheer beauty of its world-building—from ruined cities overtaken by nature to the quiet, human moments that ground its epic scale. For a series based on a beloved game, The Last of Us achieved something rare: it pleased longtime fans and converted new ones, earning critical acclaim and 20+ nominations across categories.

The Diplomat (Netflix) enters the race as a geopolitical thriller that surprises with its emotional intelligence and razor-sharp writing. Created by Debora Cahn, a veteran of The West Wing and Homeland, the show stars Keri Russell as Kate Wyler, a career diplomat thrust into the global spotlight. Russell's nuanced performance anchors a show that's as much about marriage and identity as it is about international crises. The Diplomat thrives on its fast-paced dialogue, political intrigue, and the emotional toll of leadership. It also benefits from strong ensemble work and deft direction, making it one of the year's most intelligent—and bingeable—dramas.

Another critically acclaimed nominee is Slow Horses (Apple TV+), a British spy drama that has steadily built a devoted following. Starring Gary Oldman in a career-redefining television role, the show follows a group of disgraced MI5 agents relegated to bureaucratic exile. What sets Slow Horses apart is its unglamorous depiction of espionage. Gone are the slick gadgets and high-octane chases; instead, viewers get crumbling office buildings, messy politics, and psychological chess games. The writing is sharp, the pacing tight, and the character development exceptional. With each season, Slow Horses has deepened its intrigue while keeping its cynical wit intact. It's a quiet powerhouse in a sea of louder contenders.

One of the season's most intriguing inclusions is Andor (Disney+), a Star Wars prequel series that defies franchise expectations. Created by Tony Gilroy, Andor tells the story of Cassian Andor before the events of Rogue One, but it plays less like a space opera and more like a grounded political drama. The show's mature themes—resistance, radicalization, oppression—resonate deeply, offering a rare meditation on rebellion in a galaxy far, far away. It's a risk for a franchise often associated with spectacle over substance, but Andor delivers both. The performances, particularly from Diego Luna and Stellan Skarsgård, are top-tier, and the writing is among the most refined in the Star Wars universe. For voters, Andor represents the unexpected: prestige within pulp, poetry within genre.

Paradise (Amazon Prime Video) is another surprise entry, set in a fictional African republic grappling with authoritarianism, foreign intervention, and generational trauma. The series is beautifully acted, politically charged, and gorgeously shot. Led by Sterling K. Brown, who also earned a Lead Actor nod, Paradise brings international flavor and moral complexity to the Emmys. Its nomination signals the growing recognition of globally resonant stories that challenge Western perspectives and highlight underrepresented voices. As streaming continues to internationalize content, Paradise stands as a milestone—a reminder that powerful storytelling transcends geography.

Finally, The Pitt (Showtime) closes out the drama category with a dark, psychological exploration of a university rocked by scandal and violence. Featuring a standout performance by Noah Wyle, The Pitt is atmospheric, unsettling, and thought-provoking. While not as flashy as its fellow nominees, its emotional weight and thematic depth have earned it critical praise. It represents the kind of slow-burn drama that rewards patience and close viewing—perfect Emmy bait for voters who value narrative nuance.

Together, these nominees reflect a new golden era for television drama—one defined by artistic risk, political consciousness, and emotional truth. Whether through high-concept sci-fi, grounded realism, or international thrillers, this year's dramas push audiences to reflect on the world and themselves. They demand attention, provoke conversation, and linger in the imagination long after the credits roll.

What's more, these series showcase the global nature of today's TV ecosystem. From the British grit of Slow Horses to the African intrigue of Paradise, and the intergalactic rebellion of Andor, storytelling in 2025 isn't confined by borders or tradition. It's diverse in every sense—geographically, culturally, and narratively. The Emmys have often been criticized for favoring familiar names and formulas, but this year's lineup offers hope that the institution is evolving alongside its audience.

The battle for Best Drama Series in 2025 is not just a competition of production value or critical acclaim. It's a contest of ideas, of vision, of meaning. Each show in the category brings something unique to the table—a fresh voice, a new style, a different worldview. And while only one will take home the trophy, each nominee has already achieved something rare: they've elevated television into something more than entertainment. They've made it art.

Chapter 3

Laughing with Depth — The New Age of Comedy

Comedy, long perceived as the lighter sibling to television drama, has undergone a profound evolution over the past decade—and the 2025 Primetime Emmy nominations are living proof. This year's Outstanding Comedy Series lineup showcases a new era of TV storytelling: one where humor doesn't shy away from grief, awkwardness, trauma, or complexity. Shows like The Bear, Abbott Elementary, Shrinking, Only Murders in the Building, and Poker Face have rewritten the rules of what qualifies as comedy, turning the genre into a nuanced space for layered emotions, social commentary, and unforgettable characters.

Perhaps the most significant bellwether of this transformation is The Bear (Hulu), which continues to make waves as both a critical darling and cultural phenomenon. Initially conceived as a comedy-drama hybrid, the show's second season leans deeper into both genres—delivering some of the most emotionally charged episodes in recent TV history while retaining its darkly comic edge. Centered around Carmy Berzatto, a young chef trying to transform his late brother's sandwich shop into a fine dining establishment, The Bear explores the chaos of culinary ambition and the fragility of human connection.

While the series is filled with rapid-fire banter and absurd kitchen antics, its humor is rooted in truth: the kind of uncomfortable, relatable comedy that arises from stress, failure, and dysfunction. Jeremy Allen White's performance as Carmy anchors the show in a kind of frayed sincerity, while Ayo Edebiri, Ebon Moss-Bachrach, and a stellar supporting cast bring their own mix of chaos and heart. One of the most talked-about episodes of the season, "Forks," is emblematic of this new comedy era—it's simultaneously hilarious and heartbreaking, intimate and explosive.

On the other end of the tonal spectrum is Abbott Elementary (ABC), a traditional network sitcom with modern flair. Created by and starring Quinta Brunson, Abbott continues to prove that conventional format doesn't mean conventional thinking. The mockumentary-style comedy about underfunded Philadelphia public school teachers is both sharp and heartwarming, skewering bureaucracy and celebrating educators without veering into sentimentality. Its Emmy nods—including Outstanding Comedy Series and acting nominations for Brunson, Tyler James Williams, and Sheryl Lee Ralph—are a testament to its ability to entertain while tackling real issues in education, race, and community dynamics.

What sets Abbott Elementary apart is its balance. It invites laughter without cynicism. It delivers social commentary without self-righteousness. In many ways, it's the bridge between classic sitcom structure and the genre-bending tone of today's streaming comedies. It also represents an important shift in whose stories are being told. The overwhelmingly Black cast and creators give the show a voice that feels authentic, refreshing, and necessary in a landscape still playing catch-up with representation.

Another notable nominee is Shrinking (Apple TV+), a deeply human comedy about grief, healing, and the awkward process of moving forward. Created by Brett Goldstein, Bill Lawrence, and Jason Segel, the show centers on a therapist (Segel) who, following the death of his wife, begins to break the rules by telling his clients exactly what he thinks. The result is a heartfelt, unpredictable journey through loss and love—with hilarious detours along the way.

Shrinking shines in how it blends therapeutic themes with sitcom rhythms. Harrison Ford, in one of his most charming late-career roles, plays a cranky senior therapist who becomes an unlikely mentor. Jessica Williams delivers a breakout performance that balances vulnerability with razor-sharp comedic timing. The writing is witty and soulful, never shying away from the emotional messiness of its characters. It's comedy at its most generous—less about punchlines, more about presence and perspective.

Streaming platforms, again, have taken center stage in the comedy conversation, allowing shows to push form and content in new directions. Only Murders in the Building (Hulu) returns to Emmy recognition with its third season, offering another round of mystery, meta-humor, and generational charm. Steve Martin, Martin Short, and Selena Gomez continue to play off each other with effortless chemistry, while the series experiments with theatrical elements and murder-mystery conventions in increasingly bold ways.

What makes Only Murders noteworthy is how it functions as a love letter to storytelling itself. Each season feels like an intricate puzzle, not just in plot but in structure—episodes play with narration, flashbacks, and even musical numbers. Yet the heart of the show remains in its characters: three loners brought together by their shared obsession with true crime and their desperate need for connection. Comedy here becomes the bridge between alienation and belonging.

Adding a new flavor to the mix is Poker Face (Peacock), a procedural throwback with a modern twist, created by Knives Out director Rian Johnson. Starring Natasha Lyonne as Charlie Cale—a woman with an uncanny ability to detect lies—the show blends Columbo-style mystery-of-the-week plots with offbeat humor and philosophical musings. Lyonne's gravelly charm and wisecracking introspection give the show a unique tone that's hard to define but impossible to ignore. Its Emmy nomination signals a growing appetite for genre-blending comedies that defy conventional categorization.

Beyond the major contenders, comedy in 2025 is marked by risk-taking and rule-breaking. Shows like Reservation Dogs (FX on Hulu), though not in the top Comedy Series category, continue to win acclaim for their fearless writing and cultural specificity. Created by Sterlin Harjo and Taika Waititi, Reservation Dogs has carved a niche for Indigenous storytelling told with humor, sorrow, and spiritual wisdom. Similarly, I'm a Virgo (Prime Video), a surreal coming-of-age satire from Boots Riley, plays with absurdity and magical realism while tackling race and capitalism with fearless energy.

The redefinition of comedy is not just a matter of tone—it's also a matter of space. The streaming era has allowed comedy to escape rigid time slots and ratings-driven formulas. Writers are experimenting with episode length, visual style, and structure. Comedies are now just as likely to be 50-minute meditations on loss as they are 22-minute laugh machines. The 2025 Emmy nominations recognize that there's no longer a single definition of funny.

This shift is not without its controversies. Some traditionalists argue that many of today's "comedies" aren't funny enough to earn the title. Others question whether hybrid shows belong in the same category as more straightforward sitcoms. But these debates often miss the point: the evolution of comedy reflects the evolution of the audience. Viewers are drawn to stories that feel emotionally honest, tonally rich, and socially aware. They want to laugh—but they also want to feel.

At the same time, comedy's power as a social tool remains as potent as ever. Whether it's Abbott Elementary's take on underfunded schools, Shrinking's portrayal of mental health, or The Bear's depiction of workplace toxicity, the best comedies don't avoid discomfort—they embrace it. They find humor in the cracks of everyday life, offering relief and revelation in equal measure.

The New Age of Comedy is not about abandoning laughter—it's about expanding its possibilities. It's about using humor as a way into deeper truths, and recognizing that the funniest moments often emerge from the darkest places. In 2025, the Emmy-nominated comedies don't just deliver jokes—they deliver substance. They remind us that to laugh, even through pain, is to connect with something profoundly human.

As the Emmy spotlight shines on these series, it confirms what many have long known: comedy isn't just the genre of escape—it's the genre of engagement. It reflects our world with clarity, compassion, and a necessary dose of absurdity. In the Golden Age of TV, comedy has never been more golden.

Chapter 4

The Limited Series Revolution

In recent years, the limited series format has transformed from a niche category into one of television's most prestigious storytelling avenues—and the 2025 Emmy nominations are definitive proof. Once seen as a middle ground between television and film, the limited series has evolved into a powerhouse genre, attracting A-list talent, commanding cinematic budgets, and offering audiences richly concentrated stories with profound emotional and narrative payoff. This year's nominees, including The Penguin, Monsters: The Menendez Story, Black Mirror, Lessons in Chemistry, Fargo, and Feud: Capote vs. The Swans, are not just diverse in genre but unified in ambition. Together, they represent the peak of short-form storytelling.

At the center of this limited series revolution stands HBO Max's The Penguin, a gritty spinoff from The Batman universe that surprised even die-hard comic book fans with its prestige tone and layered character study. Colin Farrell's unrecognizable transformation into Oswald Cobblepot, a.k.a. The Penguin, elevated the genre into Emmy territory. This isn't a story about villains and capes—it's a crime saga, reminiscent of The Sopranos or Boardwalk Empire, with a grounded, psychological edge. With eight episodes of tightly coiled tension, The Penguin digs deep into the psyche of its antihero, charting his bloody rise through Gotham's criminal hierarchy in a world still reeling from political vacuum and social decay.

The brilliance of The Penguin lies in its restraint. Instead of offering grand battles or CGI-fueled mayhem, it relies on sharp dialogue, character-driven plotting, and slow-burning suspense. The limited run allows the creators to build toward a powerful, focused climax without overstaying their welcome. Its Emmy-leading nominations across acting, directing, cinematography, and sound design reflect its all-around excellence, and its success signals a new direction for franchise television: concise, mature, and purposefully limited.

In contrast, Monsters: The Menendez Story (Netflix) delves into true crime, reviving the anthology's controversial exploration of real-life horror. Following the Emmy-winning success of Dahmer – Monster: The Jeffrey Dahmer Story, creator Ryan Murphy returns with another dramatized case that walks the line between exploitation and exploration. Monsters presents the Menendez brothers' story with a fresh lens, focusing on psychological trauma, parental abuse, and media sensationalism. While critics remain divided on its ethical stance, there's no denying the series' meticulous production and compelling performances, particularly from the young actors portraying Lyle and Erik Menendez.

The series' inclusion in this year's Emmy lineup points to the ongoing cultural fascination with crime and justice—and the way limited series offer the perfect canvas for deep, episodic dissections of morally complex figures. What would feel stretched across multiple seasons or rushed in a film instead finds perfect pacing in eight or ten episodes. The limited format gives space for emotional nuance while maintaining narrative urgency.

Another bold nominee is Black Mirror (Netflix), returning after a brief hiatus with a season that embraces variety, unpredictability, and eerie relevance. With standalone episodes like "Demon

79" and "Joan Is Awful," Charlie Brooker's anthology pushes its dark satire into new territories. "Joan Is Awful" in particular—about an average woman who discovers her life is being streamed live as content—earned writing and acting nominations and sparked widespread online debate. Though the episodes differ in tone and setting, the season's unifying theme is the commodification of identity in an algorithm-driven world. As with previous seasons, Black Mirror once again forces viewers to confront the dark intersections between technology and humanity.

What makes Black Mirror distinct in the limited series category is its refusal to follow conventional arcs. Each episode functions as a self-contained parable—complete with its own aesthetic, cast, and climax. This modular approach defies linear storytelling yet still creates cumulative impact. It's a masterclass in how the limited structure can liberate creativity rather than restrict it.

On the more traditional side, Lessons in Chemistry (Apple TV+), based on the bestselling novel by Bonnie Garmus, tells the story of a female scientist-turned-TV cooking host in the 1950s. Starring Brie Larson, who also serves as executive producer, the series combines historical drama, feminist critique, and romance in a way that feels heartfelt rather than heavy-handed. The limited format allows the show to chart Elizabeth Zott's evolution—from a brilliant but dismissed chemist to a reluctant media personality using science to teach homemakers—in a digestible arc that's emotionally satisfying and dramatically cohesive.

Larson's performance garnered a Lead Actress nomination, and the show's lush production design and era-appropriate costuming have also been praised. More than anything, Lessons in Chemistry embodies the best of what limited series can offer: an intimate, character-driven story told with purpose and closure. No cliffhangers. No forced spinoffs. Just one complete, impactful tale.

Returning to familiar territory with new relevance is Fargo (FX on Hulu), which continues its anthology tradition of self-contained crime stories with biting Midwestern noir. The fifth season, starring Jon Hamm and Juno Temple, shifts the setting but retains the show's signature dark humor, stylized violence, and philosophical musings on morality. Each Fargo season acts as a limited series in its own right, and the 2025 entry is no exception. It explores themes of domestic abuse, identity theft, and justice with a flair for the eccentric that's both unsettling and hilarious.

The Emmys have long had a soft spot for Fargo, and this year's nods show that its inventive narrative structure and rich performances still resonate. By giving each season a self-contained arc, Fargo maintains creative freshness while building a thematic legacy. It's proof that limited series don't have to be one-offs—they can exist within broader worlds, each entry distinct yet thematically linked.

Feud: Capote vs. The Swans (FX), another anthology success, rounds out the category with a sharp, stylish depiction of literary betrayal in high society. Chronicling the fallout between Truman Capote and the New York socialites he once adored—and later exposed in scandalous fiction—the series oozes elegance and venom. With Tom Hollander as Capote and Naomi Watts, Diane Lane, and Calista Flockhart as his "Swans," the show unpacks themes of fame, trust, and creative exploitation with biting dialogue and lavish flair.

Beyond individual accolades, the surge in limited series recognition represents a deeper shift in audience behavior and creator preference. Viewers today crave storytelling that respects their time. The finite nature of limited series offers promise: no filler episodes, no declining seasons, no unfinished arcs. Meanwhile, actors and filmmakers are drawn to the format because it allows them to deliver impactful performances without the long-term commitment of traditional television.

From a production standpoint, limited series are also ideal for experimentation. Showrunners can explore niche subjects, unusual formats, or ambitious narratives that might not sustain a multi-season run. There's a freedom in the limitations—an ability to swing big without worrying about longevity.

Of course, the popularity of the limited format has also blurred lines. What begins as a miniseries sometimes morphs into a multi-season anthology. Viewers have seen this with Big Little Lies, The White Lotus, and now perhaps The Penguin, which might spawn related spin-offs. Still, the Emmys have adapted, creating space for limited series that feel both contained and expandable.

Ultimately, the 2025 Emmy nominations reveal a golden age for limited storytelling. These shows, each unique in style and subject, share one key trait: they understand the value of brevity. They know when to start, how to build, and—most importantly—when to end. In a television era defined by endless options and competing distractions, limited series have emerged as the perfect format for immersive, high-stakes, and emotionally resonant storytelling.

As the boundaries between television and cinema continue to blur, the limited series sits comfortably in the center—offering the best of both worlds. And in 2025, these series don't just limit themselves—they elevate the medium.

Chapter 5

Star Power and Breakout Performances

At the heart of every great television show lies a performance—or several—that captures the imagination and holds the audience in emotional suspension. The 2025 Primetime Emmy nominations have brought a fresh wave of talent into the spotlight, highlighting both beloved veterans and stunning newcomers who have given this television season its depth, soul, and resonance. This year's performers didn't just act; they inhabited their roles so completely that their characters became cultural talking points, emotional anchors, and in some cases, even catalysts for real-world conversations. The brilliance of 2025 television lies as much in its scripts as in the people who brought them to life.

Nowhere is this clearer than in the Drama category, where Adam Scott (Severance, Apple TV+) continues to stun audiences and critics alike with his layered performance as Mark Scout—a man whose life is split between two incompatible realities. Scott's portrayal of a corporate worker whose work self and personal self are surgically divided is as precise as it is haunting. In lesser hands, the character might seem cold or mechanical, but Scott delivers a performance brimming with micro-expressions, subtle emotional shifts, and moments of raw vulnerability that deepen the mystery of the show while humanizing its existential core.

Alongside Scott, Bella Ramsey (The Last of Us, HBO) has emerged as one of 2025's most riveting dramatic talents. As Ellie, Ramsey brought fire, wit, trauma, and fierce resilience to one of television's most demanding roles. Their chemistry with co-star Pedro Pascal helped anchor the series in emotional authenticity, even as the story traversed a post-apocalyptic wasteland. Ramsey's Emmy nomination is more than deserved—it is a recognition of a breakout performance that feels both lived-in and revolutionary. Their work marked a significant moment not just for genre television, but for the visibility of non-binary performers in leading roles.

In the Lead Actor in a Limited Series category, Colin Farrell (The Penguin, Max) has taken what could have been a gimmicky villain role and turned it into a Shakespearean tragedy. Caked in prosthetics and submerged in the moral rot of Gotham's underworld, Farrell delivers a career-defining performance—menacing, tragic, cunning, and surprisingly empathetic. His Penguin is not just a gangster but a man clawing for legitimacy in a city that rewards brutality and betrayal. It's the kind of transformation that goes beyond surface makeup and costume—it's soul-deep, magnetic, and unforgettable.

Another powerhouse in the limited series field is Brie Larson in Lessons in Chemistry (Apple TV+). As Elizabeth Zott, a brilliant but stifled chemist-turned-TV cooking host, Larson walks a delicate line between steely intelligence and emotional fragility. Her Emmy-nominated turn is both a period piece and a timely commentary on gender politics, ambition, and the cost of authenticity in a world determined to keep women quiet. Larson's performance radiates quiet rebellion; her restrained expressions, precise delivery, and burning intensity make Zott one of the year's most complex heroines.

While veterans brought gravitas, 2025 also marked the rise of breakout performers—fresh faces who emerged from relative obscurity to become central figures in television's most talked-about shows. One of the brightest examples is Ayo Edebiri, whose performance as Sydney in The Bear (Hulu) earned her a Lead Actress nomination in a comedy. Edebiri's portrayal of a driven young sous-chef navigating the chaotic world of restaurant life is electric. She captures the frenetic pace of the kitchen and the weight of creative expectation with remarkable finesse. Whether commanding a brigade of line cooks or confronting her own self-doubt, Edebiri brings an honesty and dynamism that marks the arrival of a major new talent.

In the realm of comedy, Jason Segel (Shrinking, Apple TV+) reasserted his range as a grieving therapist trying to rebuild his life through unorthodox methods. Known for lighter fare like How I Met Your Mother, Segel here delivers a performance of surprising depth. His portrayal is funny, yes—but it's also raw, desperate, and deeply human. His comedic timing is matched only by his ability to break hearts in a single line of dialogue. The series itself blends humor with emotional weight, but it's Segel who ensures that the tone never feels uneven or forced.

Also returning to the spotlight is Harrison Ford, who received a nomination for his supporting role in Shrinking. At age 82, Ford proves that charisma doesn't age. His gruff, deadpan delivery, mixed with moments of unexpected tenderness, provides the emotional backbone of the show. Ford's performance feels like a gift—a legend finding a new rhythm in a medium he's only recently begun to embrace.

In Variety and Guest Acting categories, Pedro Pascal (Saturday Night Live) and Jamie Lee Curtis (The Bear, Guest Actress) delivered unforgettable appearances. Pascal, nominated for hosting SNL, showcased his comedic flexibility and pop culture savvy in a performance that went viral for its parody of The Last of Us. Meanwhile, Curtis's brief but devastating appearance as Carmy's emotionally volatile mother in The Bear sent shockwaves through critics and viewers alike. In just one episode, she laid bare the roots of Carmy's trauma with chilling force.

Another standout in the Guest Acting category is Juno Temple, recognized for her role in Fargo Season 5. Known for her earlier, upbeat work in Ted Lasso, Temple takes a sharp turn as a housewife entangled in deceit and violence. Her range—spanning vulnerability, ferocity, and dark humor—makes her one of the year's most compelling performers in a supporting role.

In the younger cohort, Dominique Fishback earned her first nomination for Swarm (Prime Video), where she portrayed Dre, a pop-obsessed loner who descends into a violent spiral. Fishback's performance is fearless—borderline terrifying, yet tragically sympathetic. It's the kind of work that haunts viewers long after the credits roll. Her nomination signals the Emmys' increasing willingness to recognize risk-taking performances that sit outside traditional genre boundaries.

These performances, from leads to supporting to guests, illustrate a fundamental shift in what Emmy voters and audiences value in 2025: authenticity over artifice, vulnerability over vanity, character over caricature. Viewers are drawn not just to spectacle, but to portrayals that feel deeply human—even when they're set in surreal or fantastical worlds.

What also stands out in this year's acting races is the diversity of roles and identities represented. From Bella Ramsey's non-binary presence in a lead drama role to Ayo Edebiri's breakout in a space once dominated by white actors, the 2025 nominations show clear progress. And yet, there's still more work to be done. Industry-wide, conversations continue around inclusive casting, equitable pay, and representation behind the camera.

Nonetheless, it's impossible to ignore the depth, range, and emotional resonance of this year's acting nominees. These performers aren't just stars—they're storytellers, channeling their craft into characters that inspire, devastate, amuse, and illuminate. Whether it's Colin Farrell's tragic crime lord, Bella Ramsey's fearless survivor, or Ayo Edebiri's ambitious young chef, 2025 is a celebration of the actor as alchemist—transforming words into living, breathing art.

Chapter 6

Real Talk — Variety, Talk Shows, and Reality TV at the Emmys

While much of the spotlight at the Primetime Emmys tends to focus on scripted dramas and comedies, the Variety, Talk, and Reality TV categories are indispensable pillars of modern television. In 2025, these genres are not only holding their ground—they're redefining what relevance, entertainment, and cultural commentary look like in a fast-moving media landscape. From sharp political satire to soul-baring celebrity interviews and genre-pushing reality shows, this year's nominees prove that unscripted formats are more than just filler between prestige series—they are cultural forces in their own right.

At the heart of this evolution is the Variety Talk Series category, where shows like Last Week Tonight with John Oliver, The Daily Show, Late Night with Seth Meyers, The Problem with Jon

Stewart, and The Late Show with Stephen Colbert continue to set the tone for political discourse in entertainment. The genre remains largely dominated by veteran voices, but what distinguishes the 2025 season is how these hosts have adapted their formats to engage deeper, respond faster, and speak more personally to the anxieties of a global audience.

John Oliver, whose Last Week Tonight has won the category for seven consecutive years, once again secured a nomination with episodes that tackled everything from AI regulation to reproductive rights, all while maintaining his signature blend of deep research and razor wit. In an era of misinformation and media fatigue, Oliver's ability to distill complex policy into compelling television has turned his show into essential viewing. His Emmy streak remains unbroken—for now—but the landscape around him is shifting.

One of the most buzzworthy developments in 2025 was the reinvention of The Daily Show, now hosted full-time by Hasan Minhaj. After years of rotating guest hosts following Trevor Noah's departure, Minhaj brought a bold, energetic voice to the program, blending his Patriot Act-style visual storytelling with the brand's legacy of satire. His version of The Daily Show isn't just funny—it's urgent. Covering everything from campus protests to climate disinformation, Minhaj's run earned critical acclaim and a surge in younger viewership. His Emmy nod for Outstanding Host reflects this seamless transition and the genre's growing demand for authenticity over polish.

Meanwhile, Late Night with Seth Meyers has continued to refine its smart, understated voice. Meyers, often overlooked amid louder competitors, has carved a niche with segments like "A Closer Look," offering pointed political analysis in digestible, nightly doses. In a saturated space, Meyers stands out for his consistency and clear moral compass—traits that resonate in a divided and anxious cultural climate. His nomination again this year feels not just deserved, but inevitable.

In the Outstanding Scripted Variety Series category, Saturday Night Live (SNL) remains a staple. But what made this season special was a renewed sense of energy, driven by a wave of new cast members and headline-grabbing hosts like Pedro Pascal, Jennifer Lawrence, and Bad Bunny. The show's sketches on AI, Hollywood strikes, and social media addiction felt particularly sharp—proving that SNL, when firing on all cylinders, can still lead the national conversation. Pascal's episode, featuring his parody of The Last of Us, went viral and earned him a guest actor nomination—one of several that helped boost SNL's standing this year.

Outside the nightly and weekly variety circuit, the Reality TV categories have continued their own revolution. What once seemed like the wild west of unscripted content has, over time, matured into a space for serious craft and complex storytelling. This year's Outstanding Reality Competition Program nominations include RuPaul's Drag Race, The Amazing Race, Top Chef, The Traitors, and breakout favorite Squid Game: The Challenge.

Perhaps the biggest twist this season was the massive success of The Traitors (Peacock), a psychological reality game where contestants must deduce which among them are "traitors" working to secretly sabotage the group. Hosted by Alan Cumming with a delicious blend of theatrical flair and villainous charm, the show combines the paranoia of Big Brother, the strategy of Survivor, and the aesthetics of a gothic murder mystery. Its nomination—and enthusiastic critical response—signifies the appetite for reality formats that are both cerebral and performative.

On the other end of the spectrum, RuPaul's Drag Race continues to reign as the genre's most culturally influential series. Now in its 17th season, the show remains a celebration of self-expression, queer identity, and artistic competition. RuPaul's continued success in the Outstanding Host category is a testament to the franchise's staying power and its evolving ability to reflect LGBTQ+ voices with glamour, humor, and grace. What makes Drag Race unique is its intersection of pageantry and activism—each lip-sync and runway challenge carrying emotional weight and cultural significance.

Also earning nods is Squid Game: The Challenge, Netflix's high-concept reality series inspired by the South Korean hit drama. While the show faced criticism for potentially missing the satirical message of the original, its scale, design, and dramatic stakes wowed audiences. It successfully blended scripted spectacle with real-life contestants, proving that streaming platforms can innovate within the unscripted space just as powerfully as they do in drama and comedy.

In the Structured and Unstructured Reality categories, we see even more proof of reality TV's increasing depth. Shows like Queer Eye, Selena + Chef, Welcome to Wrexham, and The Kardashians all brought personal stories and aspirational narratives to the forefront. Welcome to Wrexham, in particular, earned praise not just for its fish-out-of-water tale of Ryan Reynolds and Rob McElhenney buying a Welsh football club, but for its moving exploration of community, hope, and the beauty of small-town resilience. The series blurs the line between sports doc and heartfelt documentary—a perfect fit for today's content-hungry, emotionally literate audience.

Meanwhile, The Kardashians—now in its Hulu iteration—continues to receive both scorn and admiration. While it's easy to write off the series as superficial, its nomination highlights the Emmys' understanding that cultural relevance, audience engagement, and longevity matter. The Kardashians, for better or worse, have defined an era of reality television—and their continued presence in awards conversations reflects that impact.

One major trend across all these categories is audience engagement. Unlike traditional scripted shows, variety and reality programming rely heavily on immediate interaction—memes, tweets, YouTube clips, and TikToks can make or break an episode. Shows like SNL, The Daily Show, and The

Traitors understand that virality is now a form of currency. The best unscripted content doesn't just entertain—it lives alongside the viewer, moment to moment, and adapts in real time.

And of course, these categories have provided a platform for diverse voices. From Hasan Minhaj to RuPaul to the global contestants on The Amazing Race, the 2025 nominations reflect a world that's broader, more connected, and more expressive than ever. Reality and variety programming now do more than fill time slots—they give space to stories that scripted TV can't always accommodate.

As the entertainment industry evolves, so too does our definition of excellence. The 2025 Emmy nominations show that unscripted doesn't mean unimportant. From Alan Cumming's theatrical antics in a Scottish castle to John Oliver's searing policy takedowns, the variety, talk, and reality fields have become arenas for artistry, influence, and cultural significance.

The lines between highbrow and mainstream have all but disappeared. In this Emmy chapter, real talk means real impact—and 2025's honorees prove that sometimes, the most memorable television is the kind that isn't scripted at all.

Chapter 7

Representation and Inclusion

In an era defined by cultural reckoning and social consciousness, television has increasingly taken up the mantle of reflecting and challenging the world we live in. The 2025 Primetime Emmy nominations signal an important evolution—not just in storytelling, but in who gets to tell those stories. From more inclusive casting and greater recognition of creators of color to breakthroughs for LGBTQ+ and disabled performers, this year's Emmy lineup reveals a long-overdue but encouraging shift toward equity, visibility, and authenticity.

For decades, critics have pointed to the Emmys' track record of favoring familiar faces and predominantly white, male-dominated narratives. While those patterns haven't vanished entirely, the 2025 list of nominees tells a different story—one that suggests progress is not only possible but also popular. Audiences want stories that reflect a broader spectrum of identities, experiences, and cultures, and Emmy voters seem to be listening.

A shining example of this shift is Ayo Edebiri, nominated for Lead Actress in a Comedy Series for her breakout role as Sydney Adamu in The Bear (Hulu). A Nigerian-American actress and comedian, Edebiri has captured audiences with a performance that's smart, vulnerable, and layered. Her portrayal of a young Black woman navigating the high-stakes culinary world in Chicago isn't just about cooking—it's about ambition, representation, and pressure in male-dominated spaces. Her nomination is not just a nod to talent; it's a signal that Black women are finally getting their due in complex, lead roles that go beyond stereotypes.

Equally groundbreaking is Bella Ramsey's nomination for Lead Actor in a Drama Series for The Last of Us (HBO). As a non-binary performer in one of the most-watched and critically acclaimed shows of the year, Ramsey's presence in the top drama category is a powerful statement about inclusion. Their portrayal of Ellie—a brave, fierce, and emotionally wounded teenager in a post-apocalyptic world—offered a portrayal of queer youth rarely seen on television: defiant, multi-dimensional, and deeply human. With Ellie canonically queer in the source material, Ramsey's casting and performance added authenticity to a role that resonated with millions, particularly LGBTQ+ viewers seeking representation in mainstream storytelling.

The Emmys have also made room this year for a broader international perspective. Nominations for shows like Andor (Disney+), which features a multicultural ensemble cast led by Mexican actor Diego Luna, and Paradise (Prime Video), a fictional but resonant African political drama starring Sterling K. Brown, show that American television is no longer solely the domain of white, Western narratives. Instead, the Academy is increasingly acknowledging stories that speak to global themes, cultures, and experiences.

This shift is evident not just in front of the camera, but behind it. More writers, directors, and producers of color were nominated in 2025 than in any previous year. Notably, Abbott Elementary—created by and starring Quinta Brunson—continues to thrive as a network comedy that centers the lives, humor, and struggles of Black public school teachers. The show doesn't just feature diversity—it lives it in its writing room, production team, and tone. It's smart, it's joyful, and most importantly, it's authentic.

Meanwhile, in the limited series category, Feud: Capote vs. The Swans (FX) featured a supporting cast that included trans actress Hari Nef, making waves as one of the first trans women nominated in a major acting category for a role not centered on her trans identity. It's a subtle but crucial point: true inclusion isn't about highlighting identity in every storyline—it's about allowing people from diverse backgrounds to exist in a range of roles, genres, and contexts.

LGBTQ+ representation also took a prominent place in reality and variety categories. RuPaul's Drag Race continued its dominance, earning nominations across hosting, competition program, and editing. But more importantly, its influence paved the way for The Traitors (Peacock), which featured a notably queer-friendly cast and openly gay host Alan Cumming. The normalization of LGBTQ+ presence in mainstream, non-issue-focused programming represents a new era—one where queerness is neither novelty nor controversy but simply part of the fabric of modern entertainment.

One of the most compelling indicators of progress in 2025 is the range of disabilities represented on screen. Only Murders in the Building featured a deaf character played by deaf actor James Caverly, whose inclusion wasn't framed around his disability, but rather integrated into the show's central mystery in a clever, respectful, and plot-essential way. This approach to disability representation—normalizing rather than exoticizing—is a vital step forward, and one that Emmy voters have begun to reward.

At the same time, programs like Reservation Dogs (FX on Hulu) have continued to break barriers for Indigenous representation. Although not in the top-tier categories this year, its impact lingers. The show's all-Indigenous cast, crew, and creators brought authenticity and nuance to stories long ignored or misrepresented. In many ways, the success of Reservation Dogs has opened the door for other Native and Indigenous voices to be taken seriously within the Hollywood machine.

Gender parity also saw improvement across directing and writing nominations. Women directors were nominated for standout episodes in shows like The Last of Us, Black Mirror, and

Lessons in Chemistry, while women of color like Janine Nabers (Swarm) and Francesca Sloane (Mr. & Mrs. Smith) gained recognition for writing original, genre-defying scripts. In a space where creative leadership has long been male-dominated, the presence of diverse women at the helm of Emmy-nominated shows is a welcome sign of disruption.

Still, despite these wins, the path to full equity remains a work in progress. There were still notable snubs—Asian and Indigenous actors remain underrepresented in lead categories, and Latinx performers were largely missing outside of a few ensemble nominations. The industry's efforts to expand inclusion need to continue with greater intentionality, particularly in casting and greenlighting decisions that affect whose stories get told from the start.

Importantly, the industry has begun to understand that representation isn't a checklist—it's a responsibility. When viewers see people who look like them in powerful, complex, and beloved roles, it affirms their place in the world. It fosters empathy. It builds bridges. The Emmys, as a reflection of the television landscape, have a platform not just to reward excellence—but to redefine what excellence looks like.

The audience has also changed. Today's viewers are more discerning, more globally connected, and more vocal about the stories they want to see. Social media campaigns, online think pieces, and grassroots fandoms have become powerful engines in shaping awards narratives. Shows like The Bear, The Last of Us, and Abbott Elementary didn't just earn their nominations from critics—they earned them from millions of viewers who demanded that these stories be recognized.

At its best, representation is not about tokenism—it's about expanding the creative ecosystem so that more people have a seat at the table. The 2025 Emmy nominations, while not perfect, are a clear step toward that goal. They show that the stories being honored are finally catching up with the audiences watching them.

As the industry continues to grapple with systemic inequalities, the Emmys have the opportunity to lead—not just by celebrating excellence, but by recognizing who gets to define it. And in 2025, that definition is broader, bolder, and more inclusive than ever before.

Chapter 8

The Streaming Wars

The 2025 Primetime Emmy nominations have highlighted a trend that has been reshaping the television landscape for over a decade: the undeniable dominance of streaming platforms. What began as an industry disruption has now become the norm, with Netflix, Hulu, Apple TV+, Max, Amazon Prime Video, and others leading the pack not just in quantity, but in quality. This year's nominees reflect the peak of a new era—one where digital content creators are no longer upstarts challenging traditional broadcasters, but the principal architects of prestige television.

When Emmy nominations were announced, one of the biggest headlines wasn't just who got nominated—it was which platforms triumphed. In 2025, HBO/Max, Netflix, and Apple TV+ continued their fierce battle for supremacy, with Hulu, Prime Video, Peacock, and Disney+ trailing close behind.

These companies have not only revolutionized how we watch TV—they've changed what TV is.

Take, for instance, the limited series The Penguin (Max), one of the year's most celebrated Emmy contenders. By spinning off a character from the Batman cinematic universe into an eight-episode prestige crime saga, Max (formerly HBO Max) demonstrated the power of IP when handled with storytelling finesse. This wasn't fan service—it was franchise expansion with depth and artistic integrity. The show's dark tone, grounded narrative, and outstanding performances turned it into a critical darling, showing that cinematic universes can thrive in serialized television form if executed properly.

Apple TV+, meanwhile, has firmly staked its claim as a home for quality. Its Emmy nominations this year span multiple genres: from Shrinking, a heartfelt dramedy that earned acting and writing nods, to Lessons in Chemistry, a limited series that combined historical commentary with modern resonance. Apple's secret weapon continues to be curation. Unlike other platforms that flood the market with content, Apple maintains a high bar for storytelling, betting on fewer shows with bigger impact.

Netflix, often criticized for overwhelming viewers with a firehose of new content, still commands attention when it counts. Shows like Black Mirror and Monsters: The Menendez Story drew both praise and controversy, earning Netflix a strong presence in both anthology and limited series categories. And reality hits like Squid Game: The Challenge pushed the envelope in unscripted television, proving that Netflix still has the capacity to dominate on multiple fronts—scripted, reality, and variety.

Where the streaming wars become particularly fascinating is in the tug-of-war between art and algorithm. Platforms like Netflix rely heavily on viewer data to greenlight, cancel, or renew shows. This data-driven approach has led to quick cancellations of beloved series, sparking frustration among fans. Yet, when Netflix gets it right, the result is undeniable cultural impact. Black Mirror's "Joan Is Awful" became a talking point across social media and think pieces, highlighting how the platform still knows how to tap into the zeitgeist when it counts.

Hulu, often considered the quiet contender, had a banner year with The Bear and Only Murders in the

Building—both nominated for Outstanding Comedy Series. Hulu's hybrid model (offering both network and original content) gives it unique flexibility. It's a platform that manages to house prestige while also feeding the weekly-episode release schedule, keeping conversation alive longer than the all-at-once binge model.

Amazon Prime Video made bold moves this year with high-concept entries like Swarm and Mr. & Mrs. Smith, which tested genre boundaries while exploring race, relationships, and identity. Though not all titles became critical darlings, Prime Video's commitment to ambitious storytelling—even at the risk of polarizing audiences—shows that it's willing to take the kind of creative risks that keep Emmy voters paying attention.

Peacock, a relative newcomer to the prestige game, made major strides with The Traitors, a reality competition that found surprising success with critics and fans alike. The streamer's investment in unique reality formats and comedy (including projects with veteran talent like Tina Fey and Mike Schur) signals its intentions to go beyond just being NBC's digital arm—it's here to compete.

Disney+, once hailed as a family-friendly haven for Marvel and Star Wars content, continued to struggle with its identity in the adult prestige space. While high-production values and global franchises keep the platform financially strong, its Emmy presence in 2025 was more muted. Its Marvel entries like Echo failed to match the awards appeal of past titles like WandaVision, raising questions about franchise fatigue and the limitations of IP-based storytelling when not paired with narrative risk-taking.

One of the most significant trends in 2025 is the cross-pollination of talent across platforms. Big-name actors, directors, and writers now move fluidly between services, often producing content under exclusive deals. Ryan Murphy, Shonda Rhimes, and Donald Glover have all leveraged their creative capital to deliver for Netflix, Hulu, and Amazon. This creator-first economy has made platforms less about the brand and more about who they empower.

However, the rise of streaming hasn't been without its casualties. Traditional broadcast networks like ABC, CBS, NBC, and FOX continue to struggle for Emmy recognition. While Abbott Elementary remains a breakout on ABC, few other network shows made it into top-tier categories. The networks' reliance on procedural dramas and sitcom formulas simply doesn't align with the Emmy voter's appetite for bold, auteur-driven television. Streaming platforms have the edge because they allow for narrative experimentation, freedom from censorship, and international collaboration.

Another defining feature of the streaming wars is the globalization of content. Platforms now invest heavily in international productions, and Emmy recognition is beginning to follow. Although still U.S.-centric in many ways, the Emmys are opening up to global entries—setting the stage for non-English-language shows to gain prominence. This year's limited nominations in that area suggest more progress is needed, but the infrastructure is forming.

Moreover, 2025 has seen a shift in how streaming success is measured. In the early days, subscriber numbers were king. Now, engagement metrics like completion rates, social media impact, and critical acclaim matter more. Winning Emmys isn't just about prestige—it's about brand positioning, subscriber retention, and attracting high-caliber talent. For streamers, an Emmy isn't just a trophy—it's a business asset.

Yet with all this competition, we must ask: is the streaming bubble sustainable? As platforms multiply, and subscription fatigue sets in, consolidation may be inevitable. The Warner Bros. Discovery merger and Disney's ongoing restructuring efforts show that the golden age of "more is more" may be giving way to a new chapter of streamlined, strategic curation. In that landscape, awards like the Emmys will become even more critical in shaping which shows rise above the noise.

Ultimately, the 2025 Emmys have revealed a truth we can no longer ignore: streaming platforms are now the gatekeepers of television excellence. They've democratized access to content, diversified creative leadership, and exploded the boundaries of genre and form. In doing so, they've not only won the streaming wars—they've redefined what victory even means.

As platforms continue to evolve, merge, and compete, one thing is certain: the future of television doesn't belong to those who simply stream—it belongs to those who dare to elevate the stream into art.

Chapter 9

Emmy Snubs, Surprises, and Social Media Reactions

Every year, when the Emmy nominations are announced, the list of who made the cut is only half the story. The real drama often lies in who was left out and which unexpected names crashed the party. In 2025, the announcement of the Primetime Emmy nominees ignited a digital firestorm of praise, outrage, memes, and trending hashtags. The era of passive awards show acceptance is over—thanks to social media, the public has a loud, fast-moving voice, and Emmy discourse is louder than ever.

The Snubs That Shook the Internet

The first and perhaps most glaring snub that trended within hours was the complete shutout of Yellowjackets in the major drama categories. Once hailed as one of Showtime's prestige jewels, the series received rave reviews for its sophomore season. Yet, not a single Lead Actress nomination was given to either Melanie Lynskey or Juliette Lewis—both of whom had been considered frontrunners. Twitter, Instagram, and TikTok lit up with disbelief. Fans posted side-by-side comparison clips of award-worthy performances and called out what they viewed as the Academy's blind spot when it comes to psychological horror and female-led storytelling.

Another hotly debated omission was Dominique Fishback for her fearless portrayal of Dre in Swarm (Amazon Prime Video). Her performance, a psychological deep-dive into obsession and identity, had critics calling her Emmy-worthy since the show debuted. While Swarm did receive some creative nominations, Fishback's absence in the Lead Actress in a Limited Series category raised questions about whether boundary-pushing, genre-blending roles are still too "out there" for traditional voters.

Perhaps more surprisingly, Pedro Pascal, despite having one of the most prolific years in television (The Last of Us, The Mandalorian, guest hosting SNL), was only recognized for The Last of Us in the Lead Actor category and not for his viral guest-host stint. Fans had expected him to nab multiple nominations, with many labeling his snub in Variety Guest category as "a cultural crime."

In the comedy category, Reservation Dogs was once again overlooked, despite its final season being hailed as one of the most poignant and innovative series finales in recent memory. Created by Sterlin Harjo and Taika Waititi, the Indigenous coming-of-age show has always flown under the radar in mainstream circles but is revered by critics and fans alike. Its continued absence from major Emmy categories sparked widespread discussion about how rural, Indigenous, or non-coastal stories still struggle to get the recognition they deserve in Hollywood's awards landscape.

Surprises That Made Headlines

But where there are snubs, there are also surprises—and 2025 delivered some that thrilled fans and critics alike.

One of the most unexpected and joyful twists came in the form of Jennifer Coolidge's nomination—not for The White Lotus (which ended its season last year), but for her delightful guest appearance in Abbott Elementary. In a hilarious, unhinged cameo as a substitute teacher who goes rogue, Coolidge once again proved she's Emmy gold. The nomination sparked memes and fan art overnight and reignited calls for her to become a series regular on the show.

Another pleasant surprise came in the form of The Traitors (Peacock), a reality competition show that many had initially dismissed as gimmicky. Its dark, dramatic setting, smart gameplay mechanics, and the theatrical brilliance of host Alan Cumming won over critics and audiences. Its inclusion in the Outstanding Reality Competition Program category showed that the Emmys are beginning to reward innovation in reality TV—and not just the longest-running franchises.

Even more surprising was the strong showing for Black Mirror (Netflix), which had been written off by some critics in earlier seasons for losing its edge. The anthology's 2025 return featured episodes like "Joan Is Awful," starring Annie Murphy and Salma Hayek, that combined satire, tech paranoia, and existential dread in a way that struck a cultural nerve. The show's multiple nominations, including Outstanding Writing and Lead Actress, showed that Brooker's dark vision still has bite.

And in the realm of Variety Series, Hasan Minhaj's permanent takeover of The Daily Show was met with a wave of support—and a coveted Emmy nomination. Minhaj brought new energy, millennial urgency, and visual storytelling to the legacy program, proving that a younger, more diverse voice could successfully carry the torch left by Trevor Noah. His nomination was more than a personal milestone—it was a sign that the Emmys are finally adapting to the tastes and values of a younger generation.

Social Media: The New Awards Arena

In 2025, Emmy discourse doesn't begin or end with the nominations themselves—it lives on social media, where reaction is instant, personal, and global. Twitter threads dissected categories with think-piece intensity, while TikTok creators reenacted snubbed scenes and created parody "acceptance speeches" on behalf of forgotten nominees. Instagram fan accounts turned every nomination into art, while YouTube deep dives speculated on internal Emmy politics and "who campaigned better."

What makes social media's influence so vital today is its ability to shape public perception. A nomination once mattered because it came from an esteemed institution. Now, a performance can gain prestige from virality—even if the Emmys ignore it. Shows like Beef, Jury Duty, and The Bear have benefited from post-nomination social media campaigns that reignited interest and brought in new viewers. In this climate, audience validation carries as much weight as industry recognition.

Critically, social media also becomes a space for accountability. When shows or performances by BIPOC, LGBTQ+, or disabled talent are consistently overlooked, fans and industry voices call it out in real-time. Campaigns like EmmysSoWhite or RecognizeDisabilityTalent gain traction quickly and pressure voting bodies to reevaluate their habits.

The Politics of Popularity

Behind every surprise or omission is often a layer of Emmy politics—campaign budgets, studio influence, release timing, and platform power. Some shows gain momentum through lavish For

Your Consideration (FYC) events and billboard campaigns. Others, often smaller or independent projects, rely solely on word of mouth and critical praise. As the TV landscape becomes more crowded, it's often the streaming giants with the deepest pockets who can afford to stay top of mind with voters.

This imbalance plays out in who gets seen, who gets remembered, and ultimately, who gets nominated. But it also underscores the rare victories when smaller shows like Poker Face or breakout performers like Ayo Edebiri earn nods based on merit and buzz rather than brute campaign force.

What the Snubs and Surprises Reveal

What do these snubs and surprises tell us about the Emmys in 2025? That change is happening—but not evenly. Progress is visible, especially in the increased diversity among nominees, the rise of unconventional formats, and the recognition of genre-defying performances. Yet, legacy biases linger. Prestige still often favors a certain tone, setting, and sensibility.

More importantly, the power dynamic between awards shows and audiences has shifted. The

Emmys are no longer the sole arbiters of greatness. They are one voice among many, and their legitimacy is increasingly tied to how closely they reflect the world viewers see and demand. A snub doesn't necessarily end a performer's momentum—in fact, it can ignite it.

In 2025, the Emmy conversation is less about winners and losers and more about who's being heard. And in that conversation, social media has given every viewer a seat at the table.

Chapter 10

What These Nominations Mean for the Future of TV

The 2025 Primetime Emmy nominations have not only provided a snapshot of the current state of television—they've also offered a vision of its future. With the streaming landscape evolving, representation expanding, genres merging, and storytelling reaching new creative peaks, the Emmy nods this year reflect a medium that is undergoing a seismic transformation. What we've seen in 2025 is more than a list of outstanding shows and performances; it's a cultural blueprint for what's next in television.

First and foremost, the continued dominance of streaming platforms signals that traditional TV, while still present, no longer holds the reins of creative leadership. The prestige once associated with broadcast giants like NBC, CBS, and ABC has shifted to the likes of Apple TV+, Netflix, Max, Hulu, and Prime Video. These platforms have not only the resources but the freedom to take risks—greenlighting shows that wouldn't have survived network pilot seasons. The success of series like The Bear, The Last of Us, and Lessons in Chemistry points toward an increasingly on-demand, genre-bending television future.

But this future isn't just about who produces the shows—it's about what kind of stories get told. The nominations for 2025 reflect a broader, richer narrative ecosystem than we've seen in years past. Shows led by women, LGBTQ+ individuals, and people of color are no longer relegated to niche markets—they're front and center. The industry is beginning to understand that diverse stories don't just matter morally—they matter commercially and critically. The success of Ayo Edebiri, Bella Ramsey, Quinta Brunson, and Ali Wong at this year's Emmys underscores a growing appetite for authentic, underrepresented voices in the mainstream.

This shift also impacts the types of characters we see on screen. No longer are leads confined to traditional "hero" roles or narrow archetypes. Instead, we're seeing characters that are messy, complex, vulnerable, and often unlikeable—in other words, human. Whether it's the emotionally stifled chefs in The Bear, the grieving therapist in

Shrinking, or the morally ambiguous survivors in The Last of Us, 2025's Emmy contenders show that viewers are hungry for characters who reflect the nuance of real life.

Perhaps one of the most exciting implications for the future is the elevation of genre storytelling. Sci-fi, horror, superhero narratives, and speculative fiction are no longer just guilty pleasures—they're award-worthy platforms for tackling complex themes. The Last of Us brought depth and dignity to the zombie genre, Black Mirror reclaimed its satirical edge, and The Penguin turned comic book lore into a gritty character study. As genre television continues to mature, expect to see even more Emmys go to shows that once lived on the pop-culture fringe.

The blurring of boundaries doesn't stop at genre. Form itself is evolving. Anthologies like Fargo and Black Mirror, reality hybrids like The Traitors, and docu-series like Welcome to Wrexham prove that there is no single way to tell a story anymore. This flexibility allows creators to experiment with format, episode length, visual style, and release strategy. For audiences, this means richer, more varied viewing experiences. For the industry, it means rethinking how content is judged, consumed, and rewarded.

One area to watch closely in the years ahead is the emergence of international storytelling. While 2025's Emmys still skewed toward American productions, the global success of series like Squid Game has set a precedent. With streaming platforms continuing to invest in non-English-language content, the Emmys may soon resemble the Oscars in celebrating a more globally inclusive field. Already, co-productions between American and international studios are on the rise, signaling a future where borders are far less relevant in defining what "American television" means.

Technology, too, is shaping the next era of TV. AI tools, virtual production methods, and real-time audience analytics are giving creators more power than ever. While some fear that data-driven development could dampen originality, the success of shows like Beef—which broke narrative molds and still found mass appeal—proves that creative boldness can thrive even in algorithmic environments.

Looking at the 2025 nominations, one can also anticipate an ongoing redefinition of what "comedy" and "drama" mean. Shows like The Bear defy easy categorization—it's listed as a comedy, but delivers more emotional punches than many dramas. Similarly, Barry, now concluded, mixed crime, dark humor, and psychological complexity. This genre fluidity points toward a future where television moves beyond binary labels, and awards categories may eventually evolve to reflect that.

Moreover, the relationship between creators and fans is becoming more direct and symbiotic. Social media has transformed audiences into real-time critics and campaigners, with online fandoms shaping awards narratives and renewing shows through sheer passion. Networks and streamers have begun to listen. Fan-favorite performances and social media engagement can now push a show from the margins into awards consideration. This democratization of attention means that the future of TV will likely be even more responsive—and accountable—to its viewers.

Of course, the road ahead isn't without challenges. The 2023–2024 dual writers' and actors' strikes served as a reminder that behind every great show are artists fighting for fair compensation, creative rights, and workplace protections. While the industry has largely resumed production, the ripple effects are still being felt—and they've sparked necessary conversations about AI, residuals in the streaming economy, and equitable hiring. Future Emmy conversations will no doubt include not only who made the best show, but how they were treated while making it.

Additionally, the oversaturation of content remains a double-edged sword. As platforms continue to churn out new series weekly, it's increasingly difficult for audiences—and even Emmy voters—to keep up. While this abundance offers more opportunities for new voices, it also means that some truly excellent shows are drowned in the noise. The future may see a market correction, with fewer, more focused releases becoming the standard.

Yet, despite all the noise, 2025 has proven that great television will always rise. The Emmy nominations this year have shined a light on the innovation, diversity, and ambition that define the modern TV landscape. They reveal an industry no longer bound by old formulas or outdated standards—but striving, imperfectly but sincerely, toward something more inclusive, creative, and representative.

As we look ahead, one thing is clear: the future of television belongs to the bold. To the creators who take risks. To the platforms that elevate unheard voices. To the performers who tell the truth, even through fiction. And to the viewers who demand stories that move, challenge, and inspire.

The 2025 Emmys are not just a celebration of what was—they are a signal of what's possible. A promise that the golden age of television isn't behind us, but still unfolding, screen by screen, voice by voice.

Conclusion

A Golden Moment for Television

The 2025 Primetime Emmy Awards season has proven that television is not just surviving in a fragmented, oversaturated media landscape—it's thriving. In fact, it may be more essential than ever. What once was considered a second-tier medium behind cinema has matured into the dominant cultural force shaping how we perceive the world, interact with one another, and tell our most urgent stories.

Across ten chapters, we've explored the standout performances, powerful narratives, streaming platform rivalries, behind-the-scenes shifts, and the social movements that collectively define this year's Emmy class. But what does it all amount to? It amounts to a medium that is at the height of its creative, cultural, and technological power—a moment in history where storytelling on the small screen feels anything but small.

This year's Emmy nominations captured a television landscape in transition. Genres are colliding, boundaries are dissolving, and old formulas are being rewritten by daring new voices. Whether through The Last of Us's haunting dystopia, The Bear's intimate emotional chaos, Black Mirror's disturbing modern fables, or Abbott Elementary's loving satire of public education, 2025's best television didn't just entertain—it challenged, moved, and united.

Perhaps what is most striking about the 2025 Emmys is how personal the medium has become. Unlike film, which demands a shared theatrical experience, or literature, which unfolds in solitude, television lives in our homes, our phones, and our everyday routines. These stories sit beside us during dinner, keep us company late into the night, and give us something to talk about in the morning. They reflect the messiness of our relationships, the complexity of our politics, and the beauty of our differences.

And the Emmy nominations this year reflect that intimacy. They celebrate not just big-budget epics or ratings juggernauts but deeply human storytelling—stories of queer love, racial identity, neurodivergent characters, trauma recovery, and social justice. They reveal that the more personal television gets, the more universal its impact becomes.

Importantly, the Emmys have also become a barometer for industry values. They indicate which kinds of stories the television academy is willing to elevate, which performers and creators are finally being recognized, and which blind spots persist. The 2025 lineup shows promise: increased diversity among nominees, more international and genre-bending shows breaking through, and women dominating in writing and directing categories like never before.

Yet the conversation doesn't end with the nominations or even the ceremony itself. Awards shows now live in a dialogue with audiences, thanks to social media, podcasts, reaction videos, and fan campaigns. Emmy voters may cast the ballots, but viewers now cast judgment in real time. This democratization of media criticism has created a new kind of accountability—one where fan passion, critical consensus, and internet virality can elevate or challenge a show's legacy instantly.

We also can't ignore the economic and technological context in which these stories are made. The rise of streaming platforms, the shifts in advertising models, the strikes over AI and fair pay—these are not separate from the shows we love. They shape the kinds of risks that creators can take and the kind of careers that actors and writers can build. Television has always been an art and a business, but now the tension between the two is more transparent than ever. As consumers, our choices (what we stream, skip, or support) directly influence what kind of TV gets made.

In many ways, the Emmys represent the tip of the iceberg—the visible reward for thousands of unseen hours of labor, creativity, negotiation, rewriting, reshooting, and dreaming. For every actor walking the red carpet, there are editors, gaffers, costume designers, production assistants, and story consultants whose fingerprints are all over the final product. The 2025 Emmy season, then, isn't just about celebrity recognition. It's about honoring the collaborative, labor-intensive magic of creating art that millions of people absorb into their daily lives.

Looking ahead, the biggest takeaway from this Emmy season may be this: there is no single formula for success anymore. Gone are the days when awards went only to network dramas or big-name stars. Now, a small streaming comedy about kitchen life (The Bear) can become the cultural lightning rod. A reality competition show hosted in a Scottish castle (The Traitors) can be praised as innovative TV. A teenage post-apocalyptic survivor (Ellie from The Last of Us) can be one of the most resonant characters of the year. Television has entered a post-genre, post-format, post-boundary phase—and it's glorious.

The Emmys, for their part, are learning to evolve with it. Slowly, but noticeably. The inclusion of nonbinary actors, international storylines, and experimental formats proves that the institution is not immovable. And while there's more progress to be made—particularly in recognizing more Asian, Indigenous, and disabled talent—the trend line is pointing toward inclusion, nuance, and bold creativity.

So what do these nominations mean for the future of TV? They mean that the door is wider open than ever—for new voices, new audiences, and new kinds of stories. They mean that prestige is no longer reserved for dramas about billionaires or detectives, but can be found in awkward silences, microaggressions, TikTok-inspired scripts, and 20-minute comedies about grief. They mean that

TV is a living, breathing art form—shaped not only by critics and executives but by the millions of people who watch, share, cry, laugh, and care.

As we celebrate the best of 2025's television, we should also be excited for what's next. The Emmy spotlight shines brightly—but it also casts long shadows of potential. Somewhere, right now, a creator is writing the pilot that will dominate next year's nominations. Somewhere, a young actor is stepping onto a set for the first time, unaware that they're about to become the next household name. Somewhere, a viewer is watching the first episode of their next favorite show—one that will change how they think, feel, or see the world.

Television, in all its forms, remains one of the most intimate and influential storytelling tools we have. And the Emmys, at their best, help us recognize not just what's popular—but what matters.

Here's to the creators who take risks.
To the platforms that believe in them.
To the fans who fight for the stories they love.
And to the future of television—one golden screen at a time.

Printed in Dunstable, United Kingdom